AF507716

80's
TRUE FREEDOM
TRUE FREDOM
MATTHEW WINTERHAWK
MATTHEW WINTERHAWK

Forewarned: The Game of Life is Rigged (And They Don't Want You to Know It)

Listen up, because what you're about to read isn't just another feel-good self-help book. This is a reality check, a wake-up call, and a slap across the face to snap you out of the illusion you've been living in. And believe me, it is an illusion one carefully crafted and maintained by people who profit off your ignorance.

They've been playing a game with you since the day you were born. The rules were written long before you got here, and guess what? They weren't written for your benefit. You're the pawn, the worker bee, the obedient little cog in a machine that runs on your willingness to believe what you're told instead of seeking to know the truth for yourself.

You're sold a dream from day one. Go to school, get a job, buy a house, work until you're too tired to enjoy it, then quietly fade away, leaving just enough behind to fund the next sucker's journey through the same meat grinder. All the while, they tell you it's called "success." They wrap it up in shiny paper and tie it with a bow, calling it "freedom" or "the American Dream." But it's a lie. It's the best-marketed scam in human history.

Belief: The Greatest Tool of Control

Let's get one thing straight: belief is their greatest weapon. They don't want you to know because knowledge is power. Knowledge is certainty, and certainty can't be controlled. Belief, on the other hand, is fragile, malleable, and easily manipulated.

They sell you beliefs because they're easier to market than truth. And why wouldn't they? It's profitable. Politicians sell you belief in their promises, knowing damn well they'll never follow through. Corporations sell you belief in their products, designed to break just in time for the next version. Religions sell you belief in salvation, but only if you follow their rules. And the education system? It sells you the belief that a piece of paper guarantees success, while they rake in billions from student debt.

You cannot know what you believe. That's the first truth they don't want you to understand. If you knew it, you wouldn't need to believe it. You don't believe in gravity; you know it exists because you experience it every day. But they can't sell you gravity. They can only sell you illusions, and those require belief.

Knowing vs. Believing: Breaking the Chains

You see, the moment you stop believing and start knowing, you become a threat. Because people who know can't be manipulated. People who know are dangerous. They don't follow the herd, they don't buy the lies, and they sure as hell don't play by the rules of a rigged game.

That's why they keep you believing. Because as long as you believe, you're controllable. You're predictable. You're obedient. They own your mind, your choices, and ultimately, your life.

You've been programmed to believe in authority, in experts, in systems that don't serve you. But what do you know? Not much, because they never taught you to seek knowledge. They taught you to memorize and regurgitate. They taught you to obey.

Hope: The Greatest Drug Ever Sold

And when belief starts to waver, they sell you hope. Oh, it's the greatest drug ever sold. Hope keeps you chasing the carrot on a stick, reaching for a tomorrow that never comes. Hope keeps you voting for the lesser of two evils. Hope keeps you loyal to systems designed to fail you.

Hope isn't belief, and it sure as hell isn't knowledge. It's a wish. It's what you do when you have nothing solid to stand on. It's a desperate desire for your belief to become reality. And they love you for it. Because as long as you're hoping, you're not knowing. And if you don't know, you're still under control.

Fear: The Ultimate Prison

Fear is the most powerful tool they have because fear is rooted in the unknown. You're not afraid of the dark; you're afraid of what might be hiding in it. You're not afraid of change; you're afraid of not knowing what comes next.

They keep you ignorant because ignorance breeds fear. And fearful people are the easiest to control. They sell you security, comfort, and protection from the unknown. But all you really needed was knowledge.

The only thing to fear is fear itself, because fear is nothing more than the absence of knowledge. You're afraid because you don't know. And they don't want you to know. Because if you did, you wouldn't be afraid, and if you're not afraid, you're no longer under their control.

How They Profit Off Your Ignorance

Look around. Billionaires profit off your willingness to believe what they already know. They know the stock market is rigged. They know the news is manufactured. They know the education system is designed to produce workers, not thinkers.

They've been playing a game you didn't even know existed, using rules they wrote themselves, and profiting off your ignorance. They know the truth about debt, taxes, healthcare, food, and money itself. And they sure as hell aren't going to tell you. Why would they? If you woke up, the game would be over.

They profit because you believe. They profit because you hope. They profit because you fear. But most of all, they profit because you don't know.

True Freedom: Breaking Out of the Matrix

If you take away one thing from this book, let it be this: True freedom is in knowing. Not believing. Not hoping. Knowing. When you know, you are no longer controlled. When you know, you see through the lies. When you know, you can't be manipulated, bought, or sold.

But it's not easy. Knowing requires questioning everything you've been taught. It requires breaking the chains of comfort and confronting your fears head-on. It requires letting go of hope and finding purpose in truth.

True freedom is breaking free from the matrix they built around you. It's understanding the game, mastering the rules, and then breaking them. It's seeing beyond the illusions and realizing that the only thing standing between you and freedom is the ignorance they worked so hard to instill in you.

This Book is Your Wake-Up Call

This book isn't for the faint of heart. It's not for the comfortable, the complacent, or the obedient. It's for the thinkers, the seekers, the ones who've always felt that something was wrong but couldn't quite put their finger on it.

It's for the ones who are ready to wake up and break free. It's for the ones who refuse to play by the rules of a rigged game. It's for those who are ready to know.

This is your wake-up call. The question is, will you answer it?

Chapter 1: The Labels That Divide Us

Ignore the Labels for Thee, Not for Me

I've lived 42 years and seen more of life than most could ever imagine. I've lived in wealth, tasted fame, and felt love in its purest form. I've traveled enough to fill two passports, seen the world through lenses most people never get to wear. I've had everything you dream of money, status, power and I've lost it all. But that wasn't the hardest part. The hardest part was realizing that none of it mattered.

I grew up in poverty, the kind you don't see on TV. Five siblings, neighborhoods where gunshots were as common as laughter, where the air was thick with struggle and survival. I lived in Black, Hispanic, and poor neighborhoods where everyone was just trying to make it through the day. And let me tell you the truth they don't want you to know: the only separation between us wasn't skin color, wasn't culture, wasn't even money. It was education and knowing the truth.

The truth that what other people think or judge means nothing to your success. The truth that the labels they put on you are chains designed to keep you in place. Ignore the labels for thee, not for me. That's the game they play. They sell you identity politics while they walk free, above it all, laughing at the chaos below.

The Adjectives That Divide Us

You're not Black. You're not White. You're not Hispanic, Asian, rich, poor, or middle class. You're a human being. Period. But they don't want you to see that. They need you divided because unity is a threat to their power. Adjectives are meant to divide, to create false hierarchies and artificial competition.

They give you identities like badges to wear, and you accept them, not realizing you're also accepting the limitations that come with them. They teach you to take pride in labels that don't belong to you. They tell you to fight for adjectives instead of fighting for your humanity. And while you're busy fighting each other, they remain above it all label-less, untouched, powerful.

"Identity" is a cage built out of words, a clever construct designed to trap you in a box that limits your potential. When you define yourself by adjectives, you allow them to control your narrative. You allow them to dictate how far you can go, what you can achieve, and who you are allowed to be.

You are not your label. You are not the color of your skin, your bank account balance, or the neighborhood you grew up in. You are not your mistakes, your past, or your circumstance. You are the sum of your choices, your will, and your knowledge.

The Separation is an Illusion

I've lived on both sides of the tracks. I've been a felon and had my rights restored. I've been rich enough to buy anything I wanted and poor enough to need food stamps. I've been judged by skin color, by criminal record, by wealth, by poverty, by fame, and by anonymity. And through it all, the truth remained: the only separation was knowledge.

The only difference between success and failure is knowing. Knowing who you are, knowing the game, and knowing the rules they don't teach you. Once you know, you're no longer bound by the labels they gave you. Once you know, you can't be controlled by their judgments or limited by their expectations.

I've seen people in the poorest neighborhoods who were freer than billionaires trapped by their own wealth. Because they knew that money wasn't freedom. They knew that freedom is the power to define yourself. And that power only comes from within.

Ignore the Labels for Thee, Not for Me

They'll sell you labels like products, packaged and marketed to keep you divided and distracted. They'll tell you to be proud of your race, your gender, your identity, but the moment you accept the label, you also accept the limitations they set for you. They'll tell you to celebrate diversity while they remain united in power.

For thee, not for me. That's their game. They want you fighting over pronouns while they pass laws that keep you powerless. They want you protesting statues while they steal your future. They want you divided by identity so you never realize that we all have the same needs.

Our Needs Are the Same

Strip away the adjectives, the labels, the identities, and what do you have left? Humans. Humans who need food, water, shelter, love, purpose, and freedom. Humans who want to be happy, safe, and fulfilled. Humans who dream, struggle, hope, and hurt just the same.

We are not divided by our differences. We are united by our needs. But they don't want you to see that. They need you divided because united, we're unstoppable. They can't control a world that refuses to be divided.

I've lived it all riches, poverty, power, weakness, fame, obscurity. I've worn every label they could put on me, and I've broken free from every box they tried to trap me in. And the truth I learned is this: Labels are prisons. Knowing is freedom.

Breaking Free

True freedom comes when you stop defining yourself by their words. When you realize that the only identity that matters is being human. When you know that your value isn't determined by your skin color, your wealth, your past, or your mistakes. When you see through the labels and refuse to be limited by them.

You break free when you stop believing in their adjectives and start knowing your own worth. You break free when you realize that identity politics are nothing more than chains wrapped in pride. You break free when you stop letting others define you.

I've lived in worlds they told me I didn't belong in. I've succeeded where they said I would fail. I've been the villain in their story and the hero in mine. I've broken every label they tried to put on me because I knew they were just words, and words only have power if you believe in them.

Believe nothing. Know everything. That's the key to freedom. That's the way out of the prison of identity.

Unity Through Humanity

We're all in this game together. The labels are illusions. The divisions are artificial. Underneath it all, we're just humans trying to survive, trying to thrive, trying to matter.

They profit from your willingness to believe the labels they create. They control you by making you defend adjectives that were never yours. But the moment you see through the illusion, the moment you realize that we're all the same beneath the words, their power disappears.

True freedom is knowing the truth: that identity is a lie, and humanity is the only reality.

This is How We Break Free

This is how we break free: by refusing to be divided, by seeing through the labels, by knowing our worth beyond adjectives. We break free by realizing that we're all humans first and that our needs are the same.

This is the truth they don't want you to know because it would make you ungovernable, unmanipulatable, and uncontrollable. This is the truth that could change the world: We are one humanity, and we are more powerful united than they could ever be divided.

Chapter 2: The Education Scam

Programming Obedient Workers, Not Thinkers

Let's get one thing straight: school isn't about education. It never was. It's about indoctrination. It's about programming you to be obedient, to follow orders, to memorize and regurgitate instead of questioning and understanding. It's about breaking your spirit just enough so you'll spend the rest of your life seeking validation from authority figures.

I know this because I lived it. They tried to program me, too. But I was too curious, too defiant, and too stubborn to accept their version of reality. I saw through the lies. I saw through the system designed to churn out workers, not thinkers. And I refused to play by their rules.

I grew up poor, in neighborhoods where the schools were more like prisons than places of learning. Teachers weren't educators they were wardens, enforcing obedience and conformity. The curriculum wasn't about knowledge it was about obedience. Sit down. Be quiet. Memorize this. Don't question it. Get the right answer or be punished.

And the right answers? They were always the answers that maintained the status quo, the answers that made you easier to control. They didn't teach me how to think. They taught me what to think. They didn't teach me how to learn. They taught me how to obey.

The Hidden Curriculum: Obedience and Conformity

The real curriculum wasn't the subjects they claimed to teach. It was obedience. It was about molding you into a worker who follows rules, respects authority, and never questions the system. It was about turning you into a cog in the machine, a pawn in their game.

They taught you to stand in line, raise your hand, and wait for permission to speak. They taught you that the teacher's word was final, that the test determined your worth, and that good behavior was more important than curiosity. They taught you to compete with your peers instead of collaborating with them.

They taught you to fear failure, to avoid risks, and to always seek approval from authority figures. They programmed you to measure your value by grades, trophies, and certificates meaningless symbols that only mattered because they said so.

But the real lesson was this: Obey, conform, and don't question the system. Because the moment you start questioning, the illusion falls apart.

Memorization vs. Understanding

They didn't teach you how to understand; they taught you how to memorize. They rewarded you for parroting back information, not for questioning it. They gave you facts to memorize, but never the tools to verify them. They made you memorize dates, formulas, and rules without ever explaining the "why" behind them.

Because if you understood the "why," you might question the authority behind it. You might challenge the narrative. You might start thinking for yourself. And that was never part of their plan.

They didn't teach you how to learn; they taught you how to comply. They didn't teach you to seek knowledge; they taught you to seek approval. And that's how they programmed you to be a worker, not a thinker.

Degrees and Debt: The Greatest Scam Ever Sold

They sold you a lie wrapped in a diploma. They told you that a degree was the key to success, the golden ticket to a better life. They told you that education was the great equalizer, that it didn't matter where you came from as long as you had that piece of paper.

But they didn't tell you the truth: It's a scam. It's a racket designed to trap you in debt and keep you working for the rest of your life. It's a business model built on selling hope to the hopeless.

They told you to go to college, to get a degree, to take out loans if you had to. They promised you a career, security, and status. But they didn't tell you that those loans would take decades to pay off. They didn't tell you that you'd be working just to pay back the cost of an education that was designed to make you a better worker, not a better thinker.

They didn't tell you that your degree was just a piece of paper that put you in line for a job working for someone who never needed one in the first place. They didn't tell you that the ones at the top never played by the rules they sold to you.

College isn't about education. It's about debt. It's about making you a slave to the system before you even get your first paycheck. They make you believe that success is tied to a diploma, but they know the truth: Success is tied to knowledge, not credentials.

Programming Obedient Workers, Not Thinkers

Think about it. Why do they make you spend 12 years in school, then another 4 in college, only to get a job where you have to be retrained anyway? Why do they teach you algebra but never financial literacy? Why do they teach you history but never the present-day reality of power, control, and corruption?

Because they don't want thinkers. They want workers. They want obedient, compliant, fearful workers who follow orders, clock in and out, and never question the system. They want consumers who spend their paychecks on products that keep the machine running.

They don't teach you how to start a business, how to invest, or how to create wealth. They teach you how to apply for a job, how to follow orders, and how to compete for promotions. They teach you how to be a better employee, not a better human.

They teach you to be a cog in their machine, not the creator of your own destiny.

Breaking Free: Unlearning to Learn

You have to unlearn what they taught you to learn the truth. You have to break free from the programming of obedience and conformity. You have to stop seeking approval from authority figures who never had your best interests at heart.

Start questioning everything. Start seeking knowledge, not credentials. Start learning to understand, not just to memorize. Start thinking for yourself instead of accepting their narrative.

Unlearn the fear of failure. It's not failure; it's growth. It's not rejection; it's redirection. It's not defeat; it's education.

Unlearn the need for approval. Your worth isn't measured by grades, titles, or certificates. Your worth is measured by your knowledge, your courage, and your ability to think for yourself.

Creating Your Own Curriculum

True education isn't found in schools. It's found in curiosity, in questions, in experiences, and in failures. It's found in the willingness to seek the truth, no matter how uncomfortable it is.

Design your own curriculum. Read books they don't assign. Learn skills they don't teach. Study truths they don't want you to know. Seek mentors who have walked the path, not teachers who just read about it.

Education isn't a classroom. It's life. Learn from the people around you, from your experiences, and from your failures. Learn from your journey, not from someone else's lesson plan.

True Freedom is Knowing

True freedom isn't found in a diploma. It's found in knowledge. Not the memorized, regurgitated facts they teach you in school, but real, lived, experienced knowledge. It's found in understanding the truth behind the lies.

True freedom is knowing that you don't need their approval, their credentials, or their validation. You need knowledge. You need courage. And you need to unlearn everything they taught you about success, worth, and identity.

This is how you break free. By knowing instead of believing. By questioning instead of obeying. By seeking truth instead of approval. This is how you break the chains of indoctrination and reclaim your mind.

Chapter 3: The Entertainment Trap

Laughing at the Truth They Don't Want You to Hear

"They call it the American Dream because you have to be asleep to believe it."
— George Carlin

The truth is always hidden in plain sight, wrapped in laughter and sold as entertainment. Comedians are the last honest people on Earth, the modern-day philosophers who tell you the truth but package it in a way that's easier to swallow. They make you laugh so you don't cry. But the joke's on you if you don't listen to the punchline.

They've been telling you the truth for decades, but you were too busy laughing to hear it. You thought they were just jokes. You thought they were just comedians. But they were prophets, warning you about the game you didn't know you were playing.

The Court Jesters of Truth

In ancient times, kings kept jesters around, not just to entertain but to tell the truth no one else dared to speak. The jester was the only one who could call out the king without losing his head, the only one who could point out the absurdity of the kingdom without facing punishment.

Today's jesters are comedians, and their kingdom is the stage. But they're not just telling jokes—they're exposing the lies you live by, the illusions you believe, and the systems that control you.

George Carlin, Ricky Gervais, Mitch Hedberg, Bill Hicks, and Richard Pryor they weren't just funny. They were truth-tellers. They were the prophets of our time, screaming the truth into microphones while the world laughed and shrugged it off as entertainment.

They showed you the absurdity of politics, the corruption of religion, the deception of media, and the stupidity of society. But you laughed, because it was easier than facing the truth. You laughed, because they made it funny. You laughed, because the alternative was to get angry, to get scared, or to wake up.

They were telling you the truth. But you were too busy laughing to hear it.

George Carlin: The Prophet of Reality

"It's a big club, and you ain't in it." — George Carlin

Carlin knew the game better than anyone, and he didn't just tell jokes—he exposed the system for what it was: a rigged game designed to keep you obedient and ignorant. He told you the truth about politics, about corporations, about education, about religion. He laid it all out, plain as day, and people laughed because they thought it was just comedy.

He told you about the illusion of choice, about how democracy is just a show to keep you believing you have control. He told you about the education scam, about how schools aren't designed to make you smart they're designed to make you obedient.

"They don't want a population of citizens capable of critical thinking... they want obedient workers, obedient workers." — George Carlin

He told you the truth, but you were too busy laughing to see the system for what it was. You were too busy laughing to realize that he was warning you.

Ricky Gervais: Laughing at Hypocrisy

"Just because you're offended doesn't mean you're right." — Ricky Gervais

Gervais mastered the art of exposing hypocrisy, of holding up a mirror to society's absurdities and forcing people to laugh at their own contradictions. He mocked the self-righteousness of the wealthy and powerful, the fake virtue of celebrities, and the absurdity of political correctness.

He told you the truth about cancel culture before you even knew what it was. He exposed the illusion of virtue that people wear like a costume, pretending to care about social issues just to look good on social media. He made you laugh at the absurdity of identity politics, at the way people cling to labels for validation and status.

"Twitter is like a noticeboard in a town square. If you don't like it, move on. You don't have to read it. That's why I put up flyers for guitar lessons in a town I don't live in." — Ricky Gervais

He exposed the hypocrisy of outrage, the way people seek offense just to feel superior. He told you the truth about the absurdity of social media, about how it's a platform for fake outrage and meaningless virtue signaling.

He made you laugh, but he was showing you the truth about society's ridiculousness. He was holding up a mirror, and you were laughing at your own reflection.

Mitch Hedberg: The Absurdity of Life
"I'm sick of following my dreams. I'm just going to ask them where they're going and hook up with them later." — Mitch Hedberg

Hedberg didn't attack the system directly. He showed you the absurdity of existence itself. His jokes were surreal, his observations bizarre, but hidden in the absurdity was a truth that people missed. He was pointing out the meaninglessness of the rat race, the futility of social norms, the emptiness of materialism.

His humor was existentialism disguised as one-liners. He showed you the absurdity of chasing dreams defined by others, the futility of conforming to society's expectations, the ridiculousness of taking life too seriously.

He didn't just make you laugh. He made you question reality itself. He made you realize that life is a joke, and the punchline is that you're the one taking it seriously.

The Truth Hidden in Jokes

They hid the truth in jokes because they knew it was the only way you'd listen. If they had said it plainly, you'd have ignored them. If they had written it in books, you wouldn't have read them. If they had shouted it from rooftops, you'd have called them crazy.

So they made you laugh instead. They told you the truth about the system, about society, about life itself, and they did it with a punchline. Because the only way to tell the truth in a world built on lies is to make it a joke.

They made you laugh so you wouldn't cry. But the truth was always there, hidden in the punchline. They were the jesters, the prophets, the truth-tellers, and you were the audience, laughing at the truth you didn't want to hear.

Breaking Free: Hearing the Truth Behind the Laughter

It's time to listen to the jokes again, this time with your eyes open. It's time to hear the truth behind the laughter. It's time to realize that they were telling you the truth all along, and the real joke was that you didn't listen.

Start questioning the punchlines. Start analyzing the jokes. Start seeing the absurdity of the system they were pointing out. Because the truth they were telling you is the truth that will set you free.

Stop laughing and start listening. Because the punchline is this: They were right. They were right about the system, about society, about everything. And the real joke is that you didn't believe them.

The Power of Comedy

Comedy is the last refuge of truth in a world built on lies. It's the last honest art form, the last place where people can tell the truth without being silenced. It's the only place where reality can be exposed, where the illusion can be shattered, where the powerful can be mocked without consequence.

That's why they made you laugh because laughter was the only way you'd hear the truth. But the time for laughing is over. The time for listening has come.

Because the truth is out there, hidden in the punchlines. And it's time to get the joke.

Chapter 4: The Political Illusion

The Left-Right Scam and the Puppet Masters Behind the Curtain

"The politicians are put there to give you the idea that you have freedom of choice. You don't. You have owners. They own you."
— George Carlin

They sold you a story, and you bought it without question. They sold you democracy, the idea that your voice matters, that your vote counts, that you have the power to shape the future. But the truth is, you're not choosing your leaders. You're choosing your masters.

You think you're voting for change, but you're just changing the names on the same crooked system. You think you're fighting for freedom, but you're just reinforcing your own slavery. They gave you a left and a right, and you thought you were choosing sides. But both wings belong to the same bird, and that bird is flying you straight into a cage.

This isn't a democracy. It's a puppet show. And the strings are being pulled by people you'll never see, people you'll never vote for, people who don't care about your needs, your rights, or your future. They care about power. They care about control. And they keep that control by making you believe you have a choice.

The Left-Right Scam

The left and the right. Red and blue. Liberal and conservative. They sold you a false dichotomy, a choice between two sides that are really just two faces of the same coin. They made you pick a team, they made you wear the colors, they made you cheer for your side and hate the other.

And you fell for it. You picked a side. You bought the merchandise. You shouted the slogans. You defended your team like your life depended on it. But the joke's on you because both teams are working for the same owners.

The left and the right are distractions. They're a circus designed to keep you fighting each other so you never look up and see the puppet masters. They make you fight over social issues, cultural wars, and identity politics, while they pass laws that strip you of your freedom, your rights, and your power.

They make you think you're fighting for justice, but you're just fighting their battles. They make you think you're voting for change, but the only change is the nameplate on the same corrupt office.

You don't have a choice. You have an illusion of choice. And they use that illusion to keep you divided, distracted, and powerless.

Divide and Conquer

They don't care who you vote for. They care that you hate the people who vote for the other guy. They don't care which party you support. They care that you think the other party is the enemy.

Because if you're fighting each other, you'll never fight them. If you're divided by party lines, by identity politics, by cultural wars, then you're too busy to see the real enemy: the system itself.

Divide and conquer. It's the oldest trick in the book, and they've perfected it. They divide you by race, by religion, by gender, by income, by education, by every label they can stick on you. They make you hate each other, fear each other, fight each other.

They sell you labels and you buy the war. You defend your identity like it's your soul, not realizing that it's just a word they made up to divide you. You fight for a side that doesn't care about you, for leaders who don't know your name, for parties that don't serve your interests.

They made you pick a team, and now they own you. And while you're fighting each other, they're robbing you blind. They're stealing your money, your rights, your future, and your power.

They don't care about left and right. They care about up and down. They care about power, and they keep it by keeping you divided.

The Puppet Masters Behind the Curtain

You think politicians run the world? They don't. They're puppets. They're mouthpieces. They're actors reading from a script written by people you'll never see. The real power doesn't wear suits and ties. It wears shadows and secrecy.

Corporations. Lobbyists. Billionaires. Banks. They run the show. They write the laws. They control the money. They fund the campaigns. They own the media. They create the narrative.

They put politicians in office to keep you distracted, to keep you thinking you have a choice, to keep you believing in the system. But the politicians don't work for you. They work for the people who paid for their campaigns, the people who control their careers, the people who own the system.

You don't elect leaders. You elect employees. And their bosses aren't you they're the corporations, the billionaires, the lobbyists who bought them. The politicians are just the front men. The real power is behind the curtain, pulling the strings.

The Illusion of Change

Every election, they sell you the same lie: This time, it's different. This time, change is coming. This time, the right guy is running. This time, your vote matters.

But nothing changes. Nothing ever changes. The wars don't stop. The debt doesn't go away. The rich get richer, the poor get poorer, and your life stays exactly the same. Because the system isn't designed to change. It's designed to maintain power.

They give you hope so you won't rebel. They give you a new face, a new voice, a new puppet to believe in, so you'll keep playing the game. They sell you change but deliver the same agenda, year after year, administration after administration.

The faces change, but the system stays the same. And they keep you believing in the illusion of change, so you never realize that the system itself is the enemy.

Breaking Free: Rejecting the Left-Right Paradigm

The first step to freedom is to reject the false choice. Stop picking sides. Stop wearing their labels. Stop fighting their battles. Stop believing in their system.

The left and the right are lies. There is no liberal and conservative. There is no Democrat and Republican. There is only power and the people they control. There is only the system and the slaves who believe in it.

Stop fighting each other. Start fighting the system. Stop hating your neighbor because they vote differently. Start seeing the strings behind the puppets. Start recognizing the real enemy: the people who profit from your division.

They can't control you if you're united. They can't divide you if you refuse to pick a side. They can't fool you if you stop believing in the illusion of choice.

True freedom is rejecting the game. True power is uniting against the puppet masters. True change is destroying the system that keeps you fighting each other.

Stop playing their game. Start creating your own. Because the only way to win a rigged game is to refuse to play.

Chapter 5: The Economic Prison

Debt Slavery and the Illusion of Wealth

They sold you a lie wrapped in dollar bills. They told you that money equals freedom, that wealth equals happiness, that success equals consumption. They told you to chase the American Dream, to work hard, to buy more, to spend more, to get more. But they didn't tell you the truth: The dream is a trap, and the money is a chain.

You're not free. You're a slave. You're not wealthy. You're in debt. You're not successful. You're a consumer. And the prison they built for you isn't made of bars and walls it's made of credit cards, loans, mortgages, and bills.

They created an economy that keeps you chasing your own tail, running in circles, working longer, spending more, borrowing more, and falling deeper into debt. They created a system where money is the master, and you are the servant. And they did it so cleverly that you don't even see the chains around your neck.

You're not free because you can't walk away. You can't stop working, you can't stop paying, you can't stop consuming, because they made you believe that money is life itself.

Debt Slavery: The Chains You Can't See

Debt isn't just money you owe. It's control. It's a chain wrapped around your neck, a shackle on your freedom, a contract of servitude that binds you to the system for the rest of your life.

They sold you debt as opportunity. They told you that loans were investments, that credit was wealth, that borrowing was success. They made you believe that debt was the path to the American Dream, while they counted the interest on your servitude.

Student loans, credit cards, mortgages, car payments, medical bills these aren't just financial obligations. They're prison sentences. They keep you working, spending, and obeying. They keep you trapped in a cycle of consumption and repayment, a hamster wheel you can never escape.

Debt isn't about money. It's about control. They know that as long as you owe, you're owned. As long as you're paying, you're working. As long as you're in debt, you're a slave to the system.

The Illusion of Wealth

They sold you wealth as consumption. They told you that having more meant being more. They taught you to measure success by the number of zeros in your bank account, the size of your house, the brand of your clothes, the price of your car.

But the wealth they sold you is an illusion, a mirage that keeps you chasing shadows. It's not wealth it's liability. It's debt wrapped in luxury. It's slavery disguised as success.

You don't own your house. The bank does. You don't own your car. The lender does. You don't own your lifestyle. Your debt does. And as long as you're paying, you're not free.

They sold you a lie: Consume more, spend more, borrow more, and you'll be happy. But all you got was stress, bills, debt, and a lifetime of servitude.

The Consumer Trap

They created an economy that depends on your consumption. It's not about creating wealth. It's about creating debt. It's not about earning. It's about spending. It's not about freedom. It's about control.

They sold you consumption as status, as identity, as fulfillment. They convinced you that buying things would make you happy, successful, and admired. They taught you to define yourself by the things you own, the products you buy, the brands you wear.

They sold you things you didn't need to impress people you didn't like, with money you didn't have. And you bought it. You bought the lie. You bought the status. You bought the debt.

And now you're trapped in a cycle of earning, spending, borrowing, and repaying. You're working for things you don't need, paying for things you don't own, and losing the freedom you never knew you had.

You're not a consumer. You're a slave. And the chains are made of plastic and paper.

The Real Currency: Time and Freedom

The greatest lie they ever told you was that money is wealth. But the real currency isn't money. It's time and freedom. It's the ability to do what you want, when you want, with whom you want. It's the power to walk away, to say no, to live on your own terms.

Time is wealth. Freedom is wealth. Money is just a tool. But they made you believe that money was the end goal, the measure of success, the purpose of life.

They trapped you in a system where you trade time for money, and then trade money for things. But the things don't make you happy, so you keep trading more time for more money, and the cycle never ends.

The more you own, the more you owe. The more you buy, the more you're trapped. The more you consume, the more you're consumed.

True wealth isn't about having more. It's about needing less. It's about breaking free from the cycle of consumption, about refusing to play the game they designed to keep you enslaved.

Breaking Free: Financial Independence

You break free when you stop chasing money and start seeking freedom. When you stop consuming and start creating. When you stop buying things and start buying time.

Financial independence isn't about being rich. It's about being free. It's about living below your means, saving more than you spend, investing in yourself instead of products. It's about breaking the chains of debt and refusing to play by their rules.

Stop buying status. Stop buying identity. Stop buying happiness. Because none of those things are for sale. They're found in freedom, in purpose, in living a life true to yourself.

True freedom is needing nothing. True wealth is contentment. True success is living on your own terms.

They can't control you if you're free. They can't enslave you if you're debt-free. They can't sell you lies if you refuse to buy.

This is how you break free. By rejecting the illusion of wealth, by refusing the debt trap, by redefining success as freedom instead of consumption.

This is how you win the game. By playing by your own rules. By refusing to be a consumer. By becoming the creator of your own life.

Chapter 6: The Media and Information Control

Propaganda Machines and Narrative Engineering

"They call it the news. But news isn't meant to inform you. It's meant to scare you. It's meant to control you. It's meant to keep you distracted while they rob you blind."
— George Carlin

They sold you information, but they never sold you the truth. They sold you stories, narratives, and headlines, carefully crafted to shape the way you think, the way you feel, and the way you see the world. They sold you news that wasn't news at all it was propaganda, engineered to manipulate your emotions and control your beliefs.

You think you're informed, but you're not. You're indoctrinated. You think you're educated, but you're not. You're programmed. You think you're free to think for yourself, but your thoughts aren't your own. They're shaped by media narratives, political agendas, and corporate interests.

The media isn't here to tell you the truth. It's here to sell you a story. It's here to create a narrative that keeps you obedient, afraid, and divided. It's here to manufacture your consent for the things they're going to do to you.

This isn't information. It's manipulation. And they're so good at it, you don't even know it's happening.

The Propaganda Machines

They call it the news, but it's not journalism. It's propaganda. It's a scripted performance designed to create an emotional response, not an intellectual one. It's not about facts. It's about feelings. It's not about truth. It's about control.

They sold you news as entertainment. They sold you opinions as facts. They sold you narratives as reality. And you believed them because they wore suits, spoke with authority, and looked like they knew what they were talking about.

They don't report news. They create narratives. They decide what you see, what you hear, and what you believe. They decide who the heroes are, who the villains are, and what the story is. They control the narrative, and the narrative controls you.

The news is a script. It's a story they write to shape your perception of reality. It's a movie they play to keep you distracted from the truth. It's a performance designed to make you believe the lies they want you to believe.

Manufacturing Consent

They manufacture your consent by controlling the narrative. They show you what they want you to see, and they hide what they don't want you to know. They repeat the same story, the same talking points, the same phrases, until you believe it without question.

They decide what's important and what isn't. They decide what's newsworthy and what gets buried. They decide what you should care about, what you should fear, and what you should ignore.

They manufacture your outrage, your sympathy, your anger, and your fear. They create the problems, the villains, the crises, and the solutions. They control the conversation, the debate, and the agenda.

They make you believe that you're informed, that you're educated, that you're knowledgeable. But you're just repeating their script. You're just playing the role they wrote for you. You're just a character in the story they're telling you.

They don't tell you what to think. They tell you what to think about. And they do it so well, you think the thoughts are your own.

The Illusion of Choice

They sold you the illusion of choice with multiple news channels, websites, and platforms. They made you believe that you were getting different perspectives, different opinions, different sources of information. But the truth is, they all read from the same script.

The same six corporations own 90% of the media, controlling everything you see, hear, and read. They decide the narrative, the message, and the agenda. They control the newspapers, the television channels, the radio stations, the magazines, and even the internet platforms.

The illusion of choice is just that an illusion. They give you left and right, liberal and conservative, mainstream and alternative. But all of them are controlled by the same corporations, the same billionaires, the same power structures.

You think you're getting different opinions, but you're just getting different versions of the same story. You think you're choosing your information, but they're choosing it for you. You think you're informed, but you're just programmed.

The news isn't meant to inform you. It's meant to control you.

Narrative Engineering

They don't just report the news. They create reality. They decide what's real, what's fake, what matters, and what doesn't. They engineer the narrative, and the narrative becomes your reality.

They create heroes and villains, victims and oppressors, good guys and bad guys. They create narratives that fit their agenda, their ideology, and their power structure. They manipulate your emotions to make you believe the story, even when it's not true.

They make you hate who they want you to hate. They make you love who they want you to love. They make you fear what they want you to fear. They make you believe what they want you to believe.

They control your reality by controlling the narrative. And as long as they control the narrative, they control you.

The Fear Machine

They keep you afraid because fear makes you obedient. Fear makes you emotional. Fear makes you irrational. Fear makes you easy to control.

They sell you fear every day, every hour, every minute. They sell you fear of the other side, fear of the enemy, fear of the unknown. They sell you fear of terrorism, fear of disease, fear of crime, fear of poverty, fear of each other.

They create crises, catastrophes, and chaos. They manufacture fear to control your emotions, to control your actions, to control your beliefs. And when you're afraid, you'll accept their solutions, their authority, and their control.

Fear is the oldest trick in the book, and they use it every day to keep you obedient, divided, and powerless.

Breaking Free: Questioning the Narrative

The first step to freedom is questioning the narrative. Stop accepting their story as truth. Stop believing their script. Stop letting them control your reality.

Question everything. Question the headlines, the stories, the experts, the statistics, and the sources. Question the agenda, the motivation, and the interests behind the news. Question the narrative, the narrative creators, and the narrative beneficiaries.

Turn off the news. Disconnect from the fear machine. Find independent sources. Seek truth, not narratives. Read books, not headlines. Listen to people, not pundits.

Learn to think for yourself. Learn to see through the lies, the manipulation, and the propaganda. Learn to control your own reality, your own thoughts, your own beliefs.

This is how you break free. By refusing to play their game, by rejecting their narrative, by seeking the truth for yourself.

This is how you win. By knowing the truth, instead of believing their lies. By seeing the puppet strings instead of watching the puppets. By taking control of your own mind, instead of letting them control it for you.

Turn off the news, and turn on your mind.

Because the truth isn't out there. It's in here.

Chapter 7: The Spiritual Battle

Religion as Control and the Power Within

"Religion is just mind control. It's a way to control the masses, to keep them obedient, to keep them in line. It's a business, a racket, a way to sell hope to the hopeless."
— George Carlin

They sold you salvation but gave you obedience. They sold you faith but gave you fear. They sold you hope but gave you control. They told you that religion was the path to heaven, the way to God, the key to eternal life. But they didn't tell you the truth: Religion is the oldest form of mind control, a system designed to keep you obedient, fearful, and powerless.

They took the most powerful force in the universe the power within you and they hid it behind rituals, rules, and dogma. They made you believe that you are powerless, that you are sinful, that you are unworthy, and that the only way to salvation is through them. They made themselves the gatekeepers of God, the middlemen between you and the divine, the rulers of your soul.

This isn't spirituality. It's control. And they've been using it to rule the world for thousands of years.

Religion as Control

Religion wasn't created to enlighten you. It was created to control you. It wasn't designed to set you free. It was designed to enslave you. It wasn't meant to empower you. It was meant to weaken you.

They told you that God is outside of you, that salvation is something you have to earn, that heaven is a reward you receive after death. They made you believe that you are powerless, and that the only way to find peace, purpose, and salvation is to obey their rules, follow their rituals, and believe their dogma.

They made you believe that you are broken. And they sold you the cure. They sold you guilt, shame, fear, and salvation. They sold you hope, forgiveness, redemption, and grace. They sold you a God who judges you, punishes you, and condemns you. And they made you believe that they were the only ones who could save you.

This isn't about God. It's about power. It's about controlling your thoughts, your actions, your beliefs, and your soul. It's about keeping you obedient, fearful, and dependent.

They sold you a God who enslaves you. But the truth is, God is freedom. And the power of God is already within you.

The Business of Selling Hope

Religion is the oldest business in the world. It's a racket, a scam, a way to sell hope to the hopeless. It's a profit machine that trades in guilt, fear, and salvation. It's a business model designed to make you dependent, obedient, and generous generous to them, that is.

They sell you heaven but demand your money. They sell you redemption but demand your obedience. They sell you salvation but demand your mind. And they've been running this scam for thousands of years.

They sell you fear, fear of hell, fear of judgment, fear of punishment, fear of sin. And then they sell you the cure confession, repentance, forgiveness, grace. But the price is obedience, submission, and control.

They sell you hope, hope of heaven, hope of salvation, hope of eternal life. But they make you believe that you're not worthy, that you're sinful, that you're broken. They sell you the dream but make you feel guilty for dreaming it.

They created the disease, and they sell you the cure. And the cure is obedience, submission, and dependence.

The Fear Machine

Fear is their greatest weapon. Fear of hell, fear of punishment, fear of sin, fear of judgment. They keep you afraid because fear makes you obedient. Fear makes you weak. Fear makes you dependent.

They taught you to fear God's judgment, to fear your own desires, to fear your own thoughts, to fear your own power. They taught you to fear freedom because freedom means taking responsibility for your own soul.

They sold you fear because fear keeps you under control. And as long as you're afraid, they own you.

The Power Within

Here's the truth they don't want you to know: You don't need them. You don't need their rituals, their rules, their dogma, or their salvation. You don't need their permission to be worthy, to be loved, to be free.

The power is already within you. The divinity is within you. The God they told you was outside of you is actually inside of you. The salvation they told you to earn is already yours. The heaven they told you to wait for is already here.

They told you that you are powerless. But the truth is, you are powerful beyond measure. You are divine, you are infinite, you are free. And they don't want you to know it because the moment you realize your own power, their power over you disappears.

You don't need to be saved. You need to wake up. You need to realize that you are already divine, already worthy, already whole. You need to realize that the power they told you to worship is the power within you.

This is the truth they've been hiding from you. This is the secret they've kept for thousands of years. This is the knowledge that will set you free.

Spirituality vs. Religion

Religion is about obedience. Spirituality is about freedom. Religion is about following rules. Spirituality is about breaking them. Religion is about fearing God. Spirituality is about knowing God.

Religion makes you dependent. Spirituality makes you powerful. Religion tells you to obey. Spirituality tells you to question. Religion tells you to wait for heaven. Spirituality tells you to create it here and now.

You don't need religion to be spiritual. You don't need dogma to find truth. You don't need rituals to be divine. You don't need rules to be worthy.

You are already spiritual. You are already divine. You are already connected to God, to the universe, to all that is. And the power of that connection is within you.

Breaking Free: Finding the Power Within

The first step to freedom is rejecting the middlemen. Rejecting the gatekeepers of God. Rejecting the rules, the rituals, the dogma, the guilt, the fear, the shame.

Find your own connection to the divine. Find your own truth. Find your own purpose. Find your own power.

Question everything. Question the dogma, the rules, the rituals, the beliefs, and the fears. Question the authority, the power, and the control. Question the story they told you.

The power is within you. It always was. And once you realize that, once you truly understand that, you become free.

This is how you break free. By finding the God within yourself. By rejecting the fear, the guilt, and the obedience. By embracing the power, the freedom, and the divinity that is already yours.

This is how you win the spiritual battle. By realizing that the only enemy was ignorance. By waking up to the truth that you are already free.

Chapter 8: The Real Power You Hold

Collective Power vs. Divide and Conquer

"You know how I define power? It's the ability to make things happen. And the more people you have behind you, the more power you have. They know this, and that's why they keep you divided."
— George Carlin

They sold you the idea that you are powerless. They made you believe that you're just one person, just one voice, just one vote, and that you can't change anything. They made you feel small, insignificant, weak. They made you believe that the problems are too big, the system is too powerful, and that nothing you do matters.

But the truth is, you are powerful beyond measure. And the only reason they keep you divided is because they're terrified of what would happen if you ever united.

You have the power. You always did. You always will. But they need you to believe that you don't, because the moment you realize your power, the game is over. The moment you see through their lies, their control disappears. The moment you unite with others, their system collapses.

This is why they divide you. This is why they sell you labels, adjectives, and identities. This is why they keep you fighting over race, gender, religion, politics, and culture. They divide you because they know that the power of the people is greater than the people in power.

Divide and Conquer: The Oldest Trick in the Book

Divide and conquer. It's the oldest trick in the book, and they've perfected it. They divide you by race, by religion, by gender, by class, by nationality, by ideology, by party, by every label they can stick on you.

They make you hate each other, fear each other, fight each other. They make you believe that your neighbor is the enemy, that the other side is the threat, that the people who look different, think different, or vote different are your opponents.

They create divisions to keep you from seeing the truth: That you're all fighting the same enemy. That you all have the same needs. That you're all in the same struggle. That the real enemy isn't your neighbor. The real enemy is the system that keeps you divided.

They create problems so they can sell you solutions. They create conflicts so they can control the outcome. They create crises so they can consolidate power. They create enemies so you never see the real oppressor.

They divide you so they can conquer you. And as long as you're divided, you're powerless.

The Power of Unity

They keep you divided because they fear your unity. They fear the day you wake up and realize that you're not each other's enemies, but each other's allies. They fear the day you stop fighting each other and start fighting them.

They fear your collective power, because united, you are unstoppable. United, you are ungovernable. United, you are free.

They know that one person can be ignored, but millions cannot. One voice can be silenced, but a chorus cannot. One vote can be dismissed, but a movement cannot. They know that the people united will never be defeated.

This is why they divide you. Because if you ever realized your collective power, their system would collapse. Their control would disappear. Their power would vanish.

They fear your unity because they know that you are the real power. You always were. You always will be.

The Illusion of Individualism

They sold you the illusion of individualism. They told you to look out for yourself, to chase your own success, to pursue your own happiness, to compete with others, to climb the ladder, to be the best, the richest, the most successful.

They taught you to see others as competitors, as obstacles, as threats. They taught you to step on others to get ahead, to fight for scraps, to hoard wealth, to protect your own interests.

They taught you to isolate yourself, to think of yourself as separate, as alone, as an individual. And they did it to make you weak.

Because they know that alone, you are powerless. Divided, you are weak. Isolated, you are vulnerable. But united, you are invincible.

They sold you individualism to keep you from realizing your collective power. They made you fight alone because they knew you'd lose. But the moment you join forces with others, the balance of power shifts.

Individualism is an illusion. It's a lie they sold you to keep you weak. Because your power isn't in standing alone. Your power is in standing together.

Labels Are Chains

They sold you identity politics because it keeps you divided. They sold you adjectives because they create tribes, factions, and enemies. They sold you labels because they know that labels are chains.

They made you define yourself by race, gender, religion, nationality, and every other adjective they could invent. They made you believe that your identity was tied to a label, and they made you fight for that label.

They made you proud of your chains. They made you fight to defend them. They made you hate others because they wore different chains. They made you fight for adjectives while they ruled over nouns humans.

Labels are prisons. Identities are traps. They make you fight each other instead of the system that enslaves you all. They make you focus on your differences instead of your shared humanity.

You are not your label. You are not your race, your gender, your religion, your nationality. You are a human being. And when you realize that, the labels lose their power.

They divide you by adjectives, but you are united by your humanity. And that is the power they fear the most.

Breaking Free: United as Humans

The first step to freedom is rejecting the labels. Rejecting the adjectives, the identities, the divisions. Rejecting the false differences and embracing the truth of your shared humanity.

Unite as humans. Not as races, not as genders, not as nationalities, not as religions, not as parties, not as tribes. Unite as humans who want freedom, justice, peace, and dignity.

Find common ground. Focus on your shared needs, your shared struggles, your shared humanity. Focus on what unites you instead of what divides you. Focus on your power instead of your differences.

Stop fighting each other. Start fighting the system. Stop seeing your neighbor as the enemy. Start seeing the system as the oppressor. Stop letting them divide you. Start uniting against them.

This is how you break free. By rejecting the labels, the divisions, and the chains. By uniting as humans, as people, as souls. By realizing that together, you are unstoppable.

This is how you win. By refusing to be divided. By standing together. By uniting your power. By becoming the force they fear the most a people united and free.

This is the real power you hold. And the moment you realize it, the game is over.

Chapter 9: Living Freely in a Controlled World

Minimalism, Detachment, and True Freedom

"The reason they call it the American Dream is because you have to be asleep to believe it."
— George Carlin

They sold you freedom as consumption. They made you believe that freedom was found in possessions, in wealth, in status, in power. They made you believe that happiness was found in things, that success was found in accumulation, that fulfillment was found in consumption.

But the truth is, you are not free because you are owned by your possessions. You are not free because you are chained to your debts, your desires, your needs, and your wants. You are not free because you are attached to things that don't matter, to illusions that keep you imprisoned.

This isn't freedom. It's slavery. And they sold it to you wrapped in the flag of independence, painted in the colors of success, branded with the logo of the American Dream.

But freedom isn't found in consumption. Freedom is found in detachment. Freedom isn't found in having more. Freedom is found in needing less. Freedom isn't found in wealth. Freedom is found in simplicity.

True freedom isn't about what you have. It's about what you can live without.

The Illusion of Success

They sold you success as accumulation. They made you believe that success was found in wealth, in power, in fame, in status. They made you chase money, luxury, recognition, and approval. They made you measure your worth by numbers bank accounts, followers, likes, shares, titles, and possessions.

They made you believe that having more means being more. But the truth is, the more you have, the more you're owned by what you have. The more you possess, the more you're possessed by your possessions. The more you accumulate, the more you're trapped by the weight of your wealth.

This isn't success. It's imprisonment. It's a gilded cage, a golden chain, a luxurious prison. It's not freedom. It's slavery disguised as success.

They sold you success as consumption, but the truth is, success is contentment. Success isn't found in having more. It's found in needing less. Success isn't about accumulation. It's about liberation.

True success is freedom. And freedom isn't found in possessions. It's found in letting go.

The Power of Minimalism

Minimalism is the art of needing less. It's the power of living simply, of letting go of possessions, of freeing yourself from the chains of consumption. It's about rejecting the illusion of success and embracing the truth of contentment.

Minimalism isn't poverty. It's freedom. It's not about having nothing. It's about needing nothing. It's not about living without. It's about living within.

Minimalism is liberation. It's the freedom to live on your own terms, to define your own success, to find happiness in experiences instead of things. It's the power to walk away, to say no, to live simply and freely.

Minimalism is power. Because the less you need, the less you're controlled. The less you consume, the less you're consumed. The less you want, the freer you become.

True freedom isn't about having more. It's about needing less.

Detachment: The Ultimate Freedom

Detachment is the art of letting go. It's the power to live without attachment, without need, without dependency. It's about being free from desires, expectations, possessions, and fears.

Detachment isn't indifference. It's independence. It's not about not caring. It's about not clinging. It's about loving without needing. It's about giving without expecting. It's about living without fearing.

Detachment is freedom because it frees you from the chains of desire, from the prison of need, from the slavery of attachment. It frees you from the fear of loss, the pain of disappointment, the burden of expectation.

Detachment is power because it makes you ungovernable, unmanipulatable, uncontrollable. It makes you invincible because you have nothing to lose, nothing to fear, nothing to protect.

True freedom is detachment. It's the power to live fully, freely, and fearlessly.

Freedom from Expectation

They sold you expectation as hope. They made you believe that happiness is found in the future, that fulfillment is found in achievement, that joy is found in reaching your goals. They made you live for tomorrow, waiting for success, hoping for happiness, striving for fulfillment.

But the truth is, expectation is a prison. It keeps you trapped in the future, chained to your desires, enslaved by your goals. It makes you live for tomorrow instead of today, for the outcome instead of the journey, for the future instead of the present.

Expectation is suffering. Because the moment you desire an outcome, you become a prisoner of that outcome. The moment you attach yourself to a goal, you become a slave to that goal. The moment you expect something to happen, you give away your power to the uncertainty of the future.

Freedom is found in detachment from expectation. It's the power to live fully in the present, to enjoy the journey without needing a destination, to act without attachment to the outcome.

True freedom is living without expectation. It's the power to live freely, fully, and fearlessly, without waiting for tomorrow, without needing an outcome, without clinging to the future.

The Art of Letting Go

Letting go isn't about losing. It's about freeing yourself. It's about releasing the need to control, the desire to possess, the fear of loss, the pain of attachment. It's about being free from expectations, possessions, desires, and fears.

Letting go is liberation. It's the power to live freely, to love without fear, to act without attachment, to exist without need. It's the art of being in the world but not of the world, of living fully without clinging to life.

Letting go is freedom. Because the moment you let go, you become unchained, unburdened, unattached. You become free to live, to love, to act, and to be.

True freedom is letting go. It's the power to live without need, without fear, without attachment. It's the power to be free, fully, and fearlessly.

Living Freely in a Controlled World

They created a world of consumption, attachment, expectation, and fear to keep you enslaved, obedient, and controlled. They made you chase things you don't need, desire things you don't want, and fear things that don't matter.

The way to break free is to need nothing. To let go of possessions, of expectations, of attachments, and of fear. To live simply, freely, and fearlessly. To find joy in experiences, in purpose, in love, and in freedom.

This is how you live freely in a controlled world. By letting go of everything they told you to want, by rejecting everything they sold you as success, by needing nothing and being everything.

This is how you win. By letting go of the game, by rejecting the rules, by living on your own terms. This is true freedom.

Conclusion: Breaking Free from the Illusion

Awakening to True Freedom and Power

"The truth is, they don't want well-informed, well-educated people capable of critical thinking. That doesn't help them. That's against their interests. They want obedient workers, obedient workers."
— George Carlin

They built a world of lies, illusions, and manipulation. They sold you a dream that was really a nightmare, a freedom that was really slavery, a happiness that was really emptiness. They made you chase shadows, fight illusions, and believe in stories that were never true.

They controlled you with fear, desire, guilt, and shame. They divided you with labels, identities, and adjectives. They enslaved you with debt, consumption, and expectation. They distracted you with entertainment, news, and narratives. They programmed you with education, religion, and culture.

They built a prison without walls, a cage without bars, a slavery without chains. And they did it so perfectly that you never even realized you were a prisoner.

But the truth is, you were never really trapped. The prison was an illusion. The chains were lies. The cage was built in your mind.
And the key to freedom was always within you.

The Illusion of Control

They made you believe that they have power. They made you fear their authority, respect their rules, obey their laws, and follow their orders. They made you believe that they controlled your life, your future, your destiny.

But the truth is, they have no power except the power you give them. They have no authority except the authority you believe in. They have no control except the control you accept.

Their power is an illusion. It's a trick, a lie, a story they told you. They control you because you believe in their power. They rule you because you obey their authority. They enslave you because you accept their control.

They control you because you believe in them. And the moment you stop believing, their power disappears. The moment you stop obeying, their authority collapses. The moment you stop fearing, their control vanishes.

Their power isn't real. It's a shadow, an illusion, a lie. And the only way to break free is to see through the illusion.

The Power of Knowing

Believe nothing. Know everything. That is the path to freedom. That is the way out of the illusion. That is the key to breaking the chains.

Belief is slavery. Knowledge is freedom. Belief makes you obedient, dependent, and weak. Knowledge makes you powerful, free, and invincible.

They control you with beliefs. Beliefs in authority, in power, in success, in happiness, in identity, in separation, in fear. They sold you beliefs to keep you ignorant, obedient, and powerless.

The way to break free is to know the truth. To know who you are, to know your power, to know your freedom, to know your humanity. To know that you are divine, infinite, and unchained.

The truth is this: You are powerful beyond measure. You are free beyond limits. You are divine beyond definition. You are the creator of your own life, the master of your own destiny, the ruler of your own world.

You are not a slave. You are not powerless. You are not controlled. You are free. You always were. You always will be.

They sold you lies. But the truth was always within you.

Breaking Free from the Illusion

The way to break free is to stop playing their game. Stop believing their lies. Stop fighting their illusions. Stop obeying their authority. Stop fearing their power.

Reject the labels. Reject the divisions, the identities, the adjectives, the separations. Reject the lies that make you fight each other, fear each other, hate each other.

Reject the beliefs. Reject the beliefs in power, in control, in authority, in obedience, in consumption, in fear, in desire, in guilt, in shame. Reject the beliefs that keep you enslaved, obedient, and powerless.

Reject the game. Refuse to play by their rules. Refuse to fight their battles. Refuse to consume their products. Refuse to follow their leaders. Refuse to live by their definitions of success, happiness, or identity.

Create your own life. Live by your own rules. Define your own success. Find your own happiness. Love without fear. Live without need. Be without apology.

This is how you break free. By refusing to believe, by refusing to obey, by refusing to play. By knowing the truth, by embracing your power, by living your freedom.

This is how you win. By walking away from the game. By rejecting the illusion. By awakening to your true power.

Awakening to True Freedom and Power

The greatest lie they ever told you was that you are powerless. The greatest truth is that you are powerful beyond measure.

They made you believe that you were small, insignificant, weak, and dependent. But the truth is, you are divine, infinite, powerful, and free. You are a creator, a master, a ruler of your own world. You are the source of your own power, the author of your own story, the architect of your own life.

You are free. Free to think, to feel, to love, to live, to be. Free to create your own world, your own reality, your own destiny. Free to define your own success, your own happiness, your own identity.

You are powerful. Powerful beyond limits, beyond fears, beyond needs, beyond beliefs. Powerful beyond illusions, beyond divisions, beyond chains, beyond control.

This is the truth they didn't want you to know. This is the secret they kept from you. This is the power they feared.

The power isn't theirs. It's yours. It always was. And the moment you realize it, the game is over.

The Beginning of Freedom

This isn't the end. It's the beginning. The beginning of your freedom. The beginning of your power. The beginning of your awakening.

This is your wake-up call. This is your invitation to break free from the illusion, to awaken to the truth, to embrace your power, to live your freedom.

This is your moment. Your moment to reject the lies, to refuse the chains, to refuse the game. Your moment to live fully, freely, and fearlessly.

This is the truth: You are free. You always were. You always will be.

The game is over. The illusion is shattered. The power is yours.

Wake up. Break free. Be free.

End of the Book: True Freedom
(Everything They Don't Want You to Know)

This is True Freedom. The truth behind the lies, the power behind the illusion, the freedom behind the chains. This is the awakening to your true power, your true freedom, your true self.

This is the end of the illusion. And the beginning of your freedom.

Acknowledgments and Final Thoughts

I'd like to thank the world. You taught me everything I needed to know. Your chaos and beauty, your cruelty and kindness, your lies and truths they showed me exactly what I was up against.

To George Carlin, Ricky Gervais, Richard Pryor, and Mitch Hedberg, the truth-tellers disguised as jesters, the prophets wrapped in punchlines, the rebels who used laughter as a weapon against ignorance and fear. You taught me to see the world for what it is, to question everything, to laugh at the absurdity, and to always speak the truth, no matter how uncomfortable it is.

You taught me that comedy isn't just humor it's honesty. And honesty is the most dangerous weapon of all.

To the people and their ways, you showed me exactly what I was up against. You showed me the illusions, the chains, the lies, the beliefs that kept you imprisoned. You showed me the power of indoctrination, the pain of ignorance, the cost of obedience, and the fear of freedom.

You showed me the truth by hiding from it. You showed me the light by living in darkness. You showed me the power of love by choosing hate. You showed me the value of truth by believing in lies.

You showed me exactly what needed to be said. And I'm saying it now.

The Philosophy of Life
Fail means First Attempt In Learning. There are no mistakes, only lessons. There are no failures, only growth. There are no endings, only beginnings.

You cannot know what you believe, and you cannot believe what you know. Belief is ignorance. Knowledge is power. Believe nothing. Know everything. That is the path to freedom.

"Es ist was es ist." It is what it is. That's how I lived my life. Moral, good, and never selfish. Never asking for more than what I deserved, earned, or needed. And always being humble and appreciating anything above that.

Life is simple. Educate forever. Love hard. As the Beatles said, "All we need is love." And clean food, clean air, clean water, and shelter.

Listen to music but hear the words. Laugh at comedy but understand we're the joke. Watch the news but see the lies. Play the game but know it's rigged.

Accountability, responsibility, and respect are worth far more than any wealth or riches that can be given. Respect is truly earned, and it can never be bought.

I don't think anyone outside of ad hominem attacks could ever say a bad thing about me. They definitely hated hearing me. Because I was always right. Not because I'm perfect, but because I saw the truth. And the truth doesn't care about feelings.

Simplicity is Sophistication

Much like da Vinci said, "Simplicity is the ultimate sophistication." The truth is simple. The illusion is complicated. The answer is easy. The question is hard. The game is complex. The way out is simple.

People are perfect, just the way they are. Like Bruno Mars said, "Just the way you are." Drop the labels. Drop the adjectives. Drop the identities. Just be. Just live. Just love.

Don't be afraid to smoke a little weed and eat a little mushies. It's not about escaping reality. It's about seeing it for what it is. It's about breaking down the walls of perception, of indoctrination, of illusion. It's about finding yourself beyond the labels, beyond the beliefs, beyond the lies.

Final Words

I love you, people. I love your flaws, your mistakes, your ignorance, your beauty, your pain, your joy. I love you because you are human. I love you because you are me. I love you because we are all the same.

I love myself. Not because I'm perfect, but because I'm real. Not because I'm flawless, but because I'm honest. Not because I'm powerful, but because I'm free.

I just wish you loved yourselves. I wish you saw your own beauty, your own power, your own divinity. I wish you knew that you are enough, that you are worthy, that you are free.

I wish you saw the truth. I wish you saw the illusion. I wish you broke free from the lies. I wish you lived your life fully, freely, and fearlessly.

This is My Gift to You

This is the truth they didn't want you to know. This is the power they tried to hide. This is the freedom they could never take away.

This is the way out. The way out of the illusion, the way out of the cage, the way out of the chains. This is the way to freedom, to power, to love, to life.

This is my gift to you. Not because I'm better, not because I'm smarter, not because I'm special. But because I saw the truth. And the truth is meant to be shared.

Take it. Use it. Live it. And most importantly, pass it on.

This is True Freedom. And it was always yours.

To My Wife, Yiyu,
Who let me pull down the curtain and joined me without the circus, even though she fought me the whole way.
Your courage, love, and strength are the greatest gifts of my life.

致我亲爱的妻子，吴依渝，
你让我拉下幕布，即使你一路反对，也还是陪我一起离开了那个没有意义的马戏团。
你的勇气、爱和坚韧，是我生命中最珍贵的礼物。

To Ricky and Ava,
I pray you listen and don't waste your lives chasing slavery the way I did.
May you find true freedom, happiness, and purpose.
May you live fully, love deeply, and walk your own path with courage and wisdom.

80's
TRUE FREEDOM
MATTHEW WINTERHAWK
TRUE FEDOM